FIDELITY IS FOR SWANS

The first selection of twenty-four poems by the finest
poetical voice of the post-war generation of English
poets.

'When the historians of poetry look for the soul in
twentieth century poets they will find it in Shänne Sands.'

Alan Schoolman

I0142334

Shänne Sands

FIDELITY IS FOR SWANS

Selected Poems By
SHÄNNE SANDS
Volume 1

❖

❖

www.footsteps.co

Fidelity Is For Swans

Footsteps Press first edition
www.footsteps.co

Cover design by Kevin Reilly and
Jackie Pascoe

Typeset by Jackie Pascoe

Set in century
ISBN 978-0-9566349-4-8

To Clare my Mother
In Memoriam

*Incidental illustrations from the original hand written
scripts*

Poems

BEND WILLOW

Bend willow to the river's face
Birds let your loose feathers fall on the river's chest -
All that man has loved the best
Will bend as the willow, fall as the feather,
To the river's grace.

Laugh to the wind willow, bend and laugh
Feathers twist to the turn of the wind
All that man had long to find
Fell from the wind in half.

Sigh in the dark willow as the night creeps
Feathers tie yourself to the dark air
All that man is he must bear
As willow you sigh, but cannot speak.

❖

CARELESS LOVE

I threw my heart to the wind -
Catch it, catch it, I cried -
The wind replied, replied -
Your heart is mine, is mine -

Torrents of rain fell down
The skies became deep black;
I called to the wind for my heart -
Give it back, give it back.

And the thunder cracked -
And the thunder cracked -

I threw my soul to the skies
To search for my absent heart
Now soul and heart depart -
And I feel wise, feel wise -

Without heart to ache for love;
Without soul to yearn for truth
Blown with the wind in the skies
Blown with my youth, my youth -

❖

THE BROKEN CLOWN

Really it was my child's toy
Thrown on the floor -
With a grin knocked off in fun -
A leg half torn with stuffing
Weakly coming out -
A bright red nose bashed in -
A broken fool dim-sighted -
Shallow with absurdity -
Tomfoolery left on the bedroom floor -

Clown's intellect was only to laugh
Nothing astute could ever touch
That wide red gap of mouth -
Or straighten those hideous legs
Bent with colour -
Broken in jest by my son's rough hand -

Really it was you; there
On the grey lino -
You as a doltish clot -
Childish with silly pranks -
All your stuffing mere wool
To keep together heart and soul -
Inconsistent and dull.
From old sentiment
I'll sew the broken leg up -
Replace the stuffing -
But it's impossible to do
Anything with that gaping mouth
And those wide sad eyes -
Filled with mirth.

❖

WHEN I WAS A BRIGHT NEW-COIN

When I was a bright new-coin -
And you were a piece of blue velvet -
Our youth was a song from the hills -
Our love was a beam from the sun -

The bird's song is done -
You fled over the hills -
I've wept in cold rooms -
And the sun's beams are black -

When I was as free as quicksilver -
And you were as brave as Running Bear -
My small feet ran beside you -
And the air was pure as truth.

When sorrow was everywhere,
We said our goodbyes to love -
And told ourselves to grow-up -
And filled our cups with acid-drops -

But when I was piece of fresh life -
And you my everlasting song -
When we had the gods to tea
And spread honey on our fingers -

Then was the world a place to live -
Our garden grew songs from seeds
And we were as one in the breeze.

❖

LEATHER AND WOOD

Christ was a man of leather and wood
Only his tomb was stone -

He was a man of earth and sea
A man who understood -

The lash from the leather
The weight of the wood -

With pain in his bones
He moved the tomb-stone

He softened the wood
He sweetened the leather -

Earth and sea he bound together
Christ was a man of nail and wood -

Only his tomb was stone -

❖

REMEMBRANCE DAY
(OR HOW WE TOOK THE HILL)

Remember us today
We breathed once -
Rambled near fields
And dug our names
Out of tall trees
Till the bark bled -

Our spirits move
Its raining -
Cold -
    Drear -
        Wet -
Upon our courage
It's raining -
Till our skins
Bleed mud -
We are 'doped'
But still brave.
Our courage
Is not broken
But we die in shame -
Home-sick and crying
Why? Why?

Bergs of frozen courage -
Melted into seas -
Shimmering ice-heaps
Cold as death
Cold as old lovers
Spiteful and cruel -
Fire without flame
Soldier without name
Dead and gone -

Soil-mountains of dead
High as Everest
Where no flags
Quicken the flesh
Decayed and torn
Born for war
Birth for death -

Dying far from home
Black and white together -
White and black together -

Yellow, white, black,
White, black, yellow.
Vietnam is a ball
Of pretty colours!

Fire leaps over death
Rain soaks-up the blood -
Soldiers get 'high on pot'
And take their turn to die.

Soil-mountains heave -
Mothers grieve
Sweethearts pray -
Children play
In the U.S.A. -

Mystical white-acts
Dance in long, long robes -
A gun-sparked dawn -
Comes to the reddened sky
Strangely soft and quiet -
Let youth out of your heavy covers Death!
Let freedom out of your
Heavy covers, Earth!

They are dead and gone -
Only old wars linger-on -
They danced on polished floors -
Touched pretty beasts -
Sang over beer-mugs -
Then fled -
Down,
    Down,
        Down,
War took us away -
From known streets -
Into rice-fields of pain
Slant-eyed girls sold us sex
Our bastards are yellow and sick
To survive, that's the trick -

Deception wears a coat
Of silver and green
Shines and deceives -
Upwards the heart yearns -

Aches to possess -
Bitten with the love-bites
Of war -
We took the hill
It's there still -
We took the hill
Like a lousy whore
We climbed and crawled
To the top
Planted our flag
Then smoked 'pot'
As the dead stank -
Down,
    Down,
        Upside down -
Back into the soil -
Cut and raw -
Full of tears
Lying alone
With an oriental whore
Flown, flown
Love is now stone
And everyone is just another whore -
White and yellow and black
Give me my body back!

Old chaos dressed in black
Answers back -
'Give me a priest's white hair -
Give me a ghost in the breeze -
Give me a dancing tree -
Blown-upwards' -

Another tomb where gas
Churns in and out, out and in -
Waiting for sin
Is the pale moon -
Oh yellow war
End soon -

Unkind and unseen
Lurks a broken dream -
White-crosses stick-out of mud -
Strange birds howl
Coming and going

Over the graves -
Chanting a war-mad song -
We take our broken hearts
And retreat into the dark.

Near old leaves white flowers -
Droop white-frail heads
So near the dead -
Who took the hill;
It's there still
Like a lousy whore
Ready to be climbed
By anyone
Who can pay
The price -

They are dead and gone
Only remember them
Their song lingers on!

❖

You Are Not The River

You are not the river
I am not the mountain
We are flesh, we are blood.

You are not the universe
I am not the infinite
We are life, we are death -

You are not the rain
I am not the ocean
We are skin, we are bone.

I take your flesh
You taste my blood
Our bones and skin
Our life and death touch.

Then an ocean fills with rain -
Infinite is the river
And a mountain grows from us.

❖

SHELLEY

A pure sunbeam in an ugly world
A mind of light a heart of love -

A poet of spirits, air and earth
Wave over sand, sand over soul -

Singing master - giver of words
Living beyond emotion, beyond death -

Immortal god of free-verse -
England's poet of eternity -

Caught, held forever against Time -
Protected by clouds, by streams -

Your name is a power held in a dream -
Unseen ghosts of all poems are yours -

Near to countless scenes of beauty -
Untouched by life's odd hates

Opened through cornfields and pastures
Shall be the gates to your name -

❖

And So I Danced

Upon Eden's velvet grass
I danced -
I saw great Adam drifting past
And Eve in her snake-trance, yawn
Upon the velvet lawn -
Life saw me spinning with delight -
Called out, dance for me -
And so I danced.

I danced out of Eden -
Thinking; It's only for awhile -
Life smiled at my youthful steps
And led me mile by mile
Away from the lawns of silk -
The never fading flowers -
Calling, dance for life -
And so I danced.

Great Adam haunted my sight,
Eve forever young, wept rain -
Again and yet again
I searched for Eden's path -
But in vain -
Life pushed me into steps of
Dancing pain,
And so I danced.

Whenever I saw a coil,
That slithered like a snake,
I'd remember Eden's warmth -
And my soul ached
With mistakes -
I danced to music of the world -
Yet Heaven's notes I heard -

From simple, small singing birds,
That circled Adam's ribs -
But life called me to dance -
And so I did -

With grief I came to Eden's gate,
It was covered by thick mist -
And only by a thousand chances -
Could I find the way back in -
Great Adam held his side

With weary hands -
Beautiful Eve moaned
In long, deep sighs -
I tried to push the gate aside -
And dance upon the velvet grass
But life called me to obey the dance,
And Eden's gate was closed -
I could not pass the creatures of the dark -
And so I danced -

❖

On Two-hours of Quiet in Sandplace Woods, Near Looe With DHN

Slow, friendly stream -
Moving with August warmth -
Your water calm and lazy
Beneath an archway
Instructed to become a bridge -

Natural and lovely -
Your soothing sounds
Your swayed grasses
And arrangement of stones
Your certain promise
Of becoming increased
And important

When with measured flow
Your knowing power,
Becomes a river.

Exchanging this quiet wood
Which you with economic strength
Travel, along narrow banks -
Covered with hazel-nut and sycamore
Bramble and nettle and peat -
Offerings from summer's growth -

As geese shelter and birds sing
As sparrow-hawks in pairs
Have as their purpose
Another bird's despair.
You, gentle stream without
Difficulty wander on.

Only in this moment,
As the flies buzz above you
And your little bridge
Is warm to touch, when the
Sun a mere filtered beam
Through a dozen trees has an
Affinity with your moving soul,
Can you exercise such
Beauty that all the air
Is suddenly possessed
Of purity -

Your purpose to move on
Not to stay -
To develop, even to bring
Drama when least expected -
Your moment is here -
Now you give pleasure for today
Pain is not your meaning.
In this bedrock wood
Your youth fresh and cool
Almost identical with love -
Closes upon the seconds
Striking them better than a clock -
Your culture is eternal
For as long as rivers are -
Your language spoken
By the flowing waters -
Your simple sounds -
Higher than intellect's
Damaged voice -
You are the principle force
Of seas -
Surrounded by no doubts -

Advance sweet stream,
Slowly, without haste -
Deeper is the river
But, your shallow waters
Bring content.

❖

Sounds

I have heard them all -
Sea-sounds and rain-sounds -
And wind-sounds -
The stalks of twisted plants whine -
And the untwining of them with its
Splintered sigh -

I have heard great trees speak -
Their branches creak aloud -
And their deep arms ache
For the breaking and forsaking
In their wooden hearts -
As their long roots
Suck-up all their leaves
May share
Of forest air.

I have heard the grasses -
Swish their green greetings -
To the moving clouds and seen -
Crowds of waiting flowers -
Look-up for drops of dew.

The huge sounds of gales -
That have voices rough
With cold and ice -
And the soft, sweet sounds -
Of sunshine falling gently
Onto gorse -

I have heard the sounds -
Of a country-side in sleep -
When hedgerows lend their shade
To slumbering mice and then
To all that hurry to stretch
Their wings -

The sounds of nature's own;
Of earth, of sea -
Talking to me of perfect birth -
Always beautiful like the nightingale call -

I have heard them all.

❖

THE RUNAWAY

Youth slipped from my palm -
'Catch me, catch me,
Catch me if you can - '

I could not run so fast -
Only remember the charm
Of that laughing runaway.

Everywhere I went far or near
'I am here, I am here
Find me, find me' -

I found not a trace
Only an echo in my ears
Of youth's song -

On windy nights when alone
'Remember me, remember me
Let me in, let me in' -

Dear runaway the game is over -
You chose to roam -
The fireside is bright as the wind blows -

❖

If Smells Are Insipid

If smells are insipid -
Then the landlady's cooked supper
Lacks frankincense -
A pole-cat scent touches the ceiling;
The room is redolent with sour pork -

If streets are named after saints -
This crabbed avenue wears no halo -
After sunset the council-house tenants
Wear a wish-washed frown -
The children mostly look like pickled peppers
And the mothers are ill-flavoured lollipops -

If sounds mean sometimes melody
The ice-cream van gives me a concert
Per minute of discordant flats -
Jarring bells help sell a thousand icy treats
The driver-musician plays road minstrel
From morning into night -
As cheap cars and motor-bikes
Add noise to noise -

If idealism comes from an intellectual mind -
Only the ghost of my dream now walks -
I cannot view this scene with intelligence -
Only a troubled stare takes in the crowd -
My reverie is cornered like the fool -
And held in chains that no-one can undo -

If the pulse-beat of the city is its people
Alas, the heart of this city is flickering to death -
Only the sea snatches the wind
And blows it across the grey cement -
Only a restless gull shrieks discontent -

Occasionally the day seems
In possession of itself
Until the newsreader tells the time -
And I feel all the seconds lost -
The whole city is up-for-sale -
There's an economy in selling cities
And tucked inside the Treasurer's pocket
Are press-cuttings from the local press
Telling of the merchandise of souls -

If cheapness speaks of poverty and debt -
This booty is the grand prize -
A million untidy, unemployed people -
Walking in the rain -
Their resistance and my own -
To adversity in cities like this...
Is to enjoy the rain -
Receiving it from Heaven, then
Washing our hands of affection and favourite spots -

We are divorced from life -
Seclusion in our walk is all
I now respect!

❖

Arise Fond Animals Of Earth

The horse must be broken -
A wild beast tamed -
Dogs utterly forsaken -
The fox forever blamed -

Cattle endlessly eaten -
Cats hungry and betrayed -
The softest creatures beaten -
The fawn and mother slayed -

Shoot the rabbits also hare -
Strip the fur of every kind -
Poison, hunt, knife and snare -
All that run with the wind -

Caged are fowl, abused and ill -
Song birds tremble on the wing -
Goats and pigs join the kill -
Gentle whales fear to sing -

Apes and monkeys left insane -
Reptiles turned to pairs of shoes -
Great white bears as carpets lain -
No victim's blood ever refused -

No requiem for elephants -
Or tears for dolphins lost -
Deaf ears to wolf's last pant -
And what a fur coat costs!

Blood is falling from their eyes -
Blood is reddening their plea
Scarlet is their quick demise -
Scarlet is their destiny -

Arise fond animals of earth
Arise and haunt evil man
Arise and take your rights of birth
Arise and breathe your earthly span

❖

EARLY MORNING NOSS MAYO

Outside the cottage door
Morning is a humid greeting -
Cold, damp air infiltrates everywhere.
Muggy dew hides a patch of orange -
Crocuses trying to open for the day -
Three primroses do better -
They thrive on damp - on wet -
Their heads are soft yellow -

A thick mist sets a dull white haze around this village.
The other cottages are barely seen
And electric-light bulbs glare into the dark morning -
Milk bottles are freezing to hold -
And small cats don't go near the river -
Which is muddy, not too high,
Almost too still as if the mist has clogged
Its route and for a while stopped it breathing -
Even a dozen of so gulls are covered with moistness -
Their wings drop tiny pearls of water into the river -
Even their cry has a damp sound -

It's February, no snow, no ice,
But across the field - high near
The woods a white frost makes
Itself understood -
As light comes, as the early morning
Becomes another day -
This world of moisture will drift
Away and a warmth fill-up every cottage;
Only the grass will hold
The dew and the river will take the
Rain in-to itself.

❖

BELSIZE PARK

I looked at the shop which sold
The little green bowls

It's still on the corner of Glenloch Road,

Where so often I would spend the hours
Such a young girl carrying flowers

Bought from the man whose flower-barrow
                    stood on yet another corner.

Then to the pavements thick with snow
Where you had written "I love you so."

Now by the pavement stands a car and
                    me in fashionable clothes

No little-green bowls and comfortable shoes.
So much did I lose.

Still from the same car's window

I look at the moon so low in the sky
And think I see a tear in his eye.

But know that the tears are in mine -

❖

NYMPHOLEPT

Between the losing of a lover -
And the rising new-moon
The Christ-seekers' Easter prayers
And Jews eating matzos

Windward my heart -

These omnivorous years
With poisoned claws, all beast,
Incline and touch my face,

Windward my heart -

Morpheus persuade me with your dreams,
Do not deprive me of sensation, because I sleep,
Appease my body for all a loveless
Mind has overlooked -
And all a nympholept soul cannot find.

Windward my heart -

To wish on the rising new-moon,
Turn my silver by an open window
In the palm of my hand,
Where I once held your softness
And did not wish on the sky's offering, but
On your eyes.

Windward my heart

❖

GRASSMERE

The world of thought is not so very faraway -
And solitude remains my only friend -
Once some other friend I knew -
Who when he spoke, such soft words,
Fell as dew upon my ears -
And every echo spoke his lines in prayer -
The hills hold his image
In their power -
When the hour is fondly timed
And once again the wind shall come
And lift my soul to his -
All shall be safe and warm within
The promise of his kiss -
'Till we find the Mecca of our dreams.
Leaving the den of silence far behind -
Nearer to the call of wildly things -
Reach not in vain for my chain of songs
For we can sing once more the chants of love.
Caged not in lost despair
Or forever lost in deathly grace
Return my spirit, return and
Smile upon my face -
The world of thought is not so very faraway
And faith is mine to own -
Yet solitude remains my only friend
I am alone -

❖

THE POET'S WORD

Between the long grass and river's edge -
Lie the poet's word, without print - unheard -
Between the tall tree and the white cloud
Stretches the poet's shroud -

Between the mind's-eye and the silence
The voice of a muse cries
To the first beams of sunrise.

Between the blank page and the black ink
Hidden is the poem's complaint -
Unlike the picture full of paint.

The poem waits -

Between the long grass and the river's edge
Unheard, is the poet's pledge -
The word without print without voice
Falls to the river's bed.

❖

CYCLONE

Fifteen-thousand leaves
Float across the island seas -

Strange dark leaves
With faces masked with grieving -

The churning-seas now calm
Shows its leaves to be brown arms -

Stiff with instant death
Taking away the island's breath -

Of life and limb turned to floating leaf
Of wasted life, a sea strewn with grief.

Tropic madness; the teasing gods reply -
To earnest prayers, from those soon to die.

Next season's rice will be a rich harvest
Torn from the mother's breast.

Sea, give me my sons again
Sea, take away my pain -

The island tides come gently to and fro -
The island tides come gently now and go.

Fifteen thousand leaves awash with sea
A lone mother wept, 'Unkind gods pity me' -

❖

In Sadness

Be thou my sight if blindness comes to me,
Be thou my hearing if my ears strike deaf.
Let thy thoughts speak for me if dumb
I should become.
And if some dread disease falls upon my bones
Let it be thy hands that soothe the wounds.

For if with joy your love I do not hold
Then well I shall be blessed
If when in death 'tis thy gaze
That leads me to my rest.

❖

COME, NIGHT

Come night,
Let you and I talk awhile -
All day I seemed half-dead,
Now, with you I shall seek new thoughts
And slowly smile -

Dear night,
Who else but you, hears my secrets -
Which other friend hides my tears for me
And wipes away my regrets
With darkness -

And then night
To madly rejoice
And fill the house with laughter -
Listen, listen to my voice, I'm happy,
You are here my night, you to dance with
Beneath the black, black sky.
You and I night -
You and I.

❖

ROY

On this bed you are my lover,
Your organs suck, spit
Exhaust themselves on my belly.
My love, bodies lie -
The great love-lie,
For in the closeness
Skin to skin
Soon you will leave this bed
Make tea and forget.

Only the tulips yellow, slowly
Dying show sadness
Your typewriter screams at me,
    "I am master"
There in a dusty corner
Covered with your jacket
Love waits crying.

❖

ARENA

Of my emotions
I built stone by stone
An arena -
Meaning in its vast circus-ring
To bring on the drama of frozen-tears
And watch a play -

A comedy of misery -
Me laughing thro' the evil-plot -
Feeling comfort even relief
From this odd communion with myself -

Filch me a clown
To think, I asked for fidelity from man -
Smooth out my lined forehead -
To think I imagined kisses
Could dwarf untruth into dark corners -

Audience, come see the play -
Join-in-audience-participation -
Listen, listen,
Soothsayers are muttering -
Out of the darkness I can hear -
'Au revoir' and the flip-flop
Of tears dripping into beer-mugs -

Fiddler join my clown -
We shall have dancing -
Fetch me a drink and I'll dance too -
With my toes burning in my shoes.

Strike-up the band
Everyone inside my arena
Is going to dance (before they die)

Excitement that's the sting -
Fiddler play -
The wedding-ring
Is a gold circle of violent passion -
Musicians do not marry -
Your fiddle-de-dee's
Will sound unhappy -
Honour desire from a distance -
As warming by a fire -
Do not burn and blister -

Rejoice at your sister's wedding
Do not go to one of your own -

But play fiddler - play -
And we shall stamp our feet -
Astonished watchers in the night
Will take fright and runaway -

Too much emotion
Is not good for the Anglo-Saxon's dream -
They play the drunkard
And the hero -
But stammer when it comes to loving -
Only their poets, songsters with T.B,
Allay the emotions into words -
Only their poets bribe the heart -
Feel pain and grieve for love -
Feel anger and talk of change -
Sing of chance and sorcery
Rise from the darkness
Make the unimportant lovely -
Turn sunlight grey
And moonlight blue
Such things poets do -

The penalty for emotion
Is murky mud thrown at your back -
The quick killing of the heart's fancy.

The decay of feeling -
Of course its murder -
Yet the fragrance comes
From the myrtle plant -
Named love -

Wear a breast-plate -
A defence for the heart
From arrows of desire -
Exile love-demons -
Be vicious with your passion -
Don't yield -
Then build your arena
Next to mine -

There is glamour in emotional dying -
Link-arms and kick your heels high -

Then take a bow one at a time -
Don't break-up the chorus line -
Kick high -
There, there
Is the sky -
Join me now in my rejoicing -
Ghosts join my party too -
The arena is full of the alive and dead -
Ghosts dance with the living -
Power to the hour -

Give me a flower -
Essence of tears -
Give me a female-cat -
Essence of ghosts -

Give me your coat
And I'll hang-it up,
With all the hang-ups
Of stale loving -
Girls stay young -
Essence of sorrow is age -
Relinquish passion -
Forever done with -
A sunbeam, gone -
Into a receptacle
Made of smooth, cold skin -
Once warm over my heart -
Pleasure mixed with demons -
Essence of brittle love -

Table-talk is over -
Into the arena go -
My lions are waiting
For their kill -

Shrivelled ghosts moan -
Essence of morbid dreams -
Swallows fly over
My un-wise loves

Rumour has it that my arena
Is a bestseller -
Come we'll go together -

And thank the guests
Essence of skill -

A tambourine is making sweet noise
Nothing destroys the calm
Of early nightfall -
Call the curtain down -
Pay-off my clown -

The arena is empty -
A tremor goes over me -
Pacify me with prayers -
Come, together we'll climb
The stairs of our transient moments,
We'll share my arena -
Increase our hurt -
Praise the play -
Then I'll watch you walk away -
Essence of good-bye -

❖

www.ingramcontent.com/pod-product-compliance
Lightning Source LLC
LaVergne TN
LVHW041210080426
835508LV00008B/883